THE IMPACT OF AWAKENING

THE IMPACT OF AWAKENING

Excerpts from the Teachings of Adyashanti

OPEN GATE SANGHA
LOS GATOS • CALIFORNIA

ACKNOWLEDGEMENTS

Cover Design: Elizabeth Rose, e.Rose Design

Cover Photo: Diane Kaye

Editing: Gina Lake, Joolz Haugen,
                  Prema Maja Rode, Annie Gray

Transcribing: Gina Lake, Hamsa Hilker,
                  Donna Landman, Mayoor Steinberg,
                  Dawn Mazur, Viveka Fitzsimmons

Logistics: Garrett Prochnow, Marc Potter

ISBN 0-9717036-0-4

For more information, contact:
Open Gate Sangha, Inc.
P.O. Box 782
Los Gatos, California 95031 USA
www.zen-satsang.org

To the light of Awakeness
that reflected back to me my own True Self through the forms of:

Arvis Justi

Jakusho Kwong Roshi

Nisargadatta Maharaj

Contents

⟶ Continued ⟵

FOREWORD

When I was a Zen monk, I learned to distinguish between "live words" and "dead words." Most of the words we read and hear are lifeless, in the sense that they're rooted in concepts and intended to appeal to the mind. Of course, such "dead words" have an important role to play on a relative level, in helping us to negotiate the world of apparent objects and people.

To point us beyond the body-mind to the Source from which this relative reality arises and in which it abides, however, we need "live words," like those we find in the teachings of the great non-dual masters and sages. The sayings of Ramana Maharshi, for example, or the Tibetan master, Tilopa, or the Third Patriarch of Zen have the power to short-circuit the mind, light up the Heart, and quicken the revelation of who we really are. In Vajrayana Buddhism, such words are called pith instructions or heart wisdom. As Jean Klein puts it, they are saturated with the perfume of the Source from which they come.

The space in which live words are spoken is called satsang—literally, "being together in Truth." When we speak Truth with one another, we're creating satsang. In this brief collection of satsang dialogues, Adyashanti reveals himself to be a master of live words. Although he trained for many years with several American Zen teachers, he does not use Zen jargon. In fact, like the great Zen masters of old, he has breached the bounds of conventional

Buddhist discourse and instead speaks directly from Being itself. His words are fresh, spontaneous, and vital.

In addition to his passionate call to awaken to our identity as the Self, rather than as the body, senses, and mind, Adyashanti puts particular emphasis on what he calls embodiment. In this, he provides a much-needed counterpoint to some contemporary teachers of Advaita Vedanta, who seem to suggest that awakening is complete after the first glimpse of Truth.

Rather, Adyashanti teaches that awakening is a never-ending process of opening and deepening, in which we're often faced with difficult old patterns and stuck places that rush to the foreground of our experience to be liberated and released. As this liberation unfolds, our lives increasingly become an expression of the unfathomable mystery we have discovered ourselves to be. The process of embodiment culminates in the elimination of any vestige of separation. Awakening continues, but there is no one who is awakened.

In the many hours I've spent with Adyashanti, I've been impressed not only by his intimacy with the subtlest and deepest levels of realization but also by his seemingly inexhaustible capacity to welcome whatever arises in satsang with empathy and love. He has a penetrating way of engaging in dialogue with people, in which layers of false understanding drop away in the radiance of awareness, leaving the freshness and clarity of the living moment. He embodies what he teaches, and his approach is truly non-dual; nothing is left out, not even the ego!

I trust that this little book will be merely the first in a series from this vibrant young teacher. May his "live words" help awaken all beings to the joy and perfection of their essential nature!

Stephan Bodian
Mill Valley, California
March 2000

Stephan Bodian is a psychotherapist, personal coach, and a Dharma teacher in the Zen tradition. He is the author of Meditation for Dummies *and former editor-in-chief of* Yoga Journal.

INTRODUCTION

When you come to the point in life where you are ready to inquire directly into the unknown core of your being, you are ripe to awaken from the dream of separation. The direct path of spiritual inquiry begins not with seeking something that you yearn for, but with seeking the seeker, the essential "I."

In order for inquiry to be powerful and liberating, it needs to be understood that spiritual inquiry is not something to be performed by the mind. Inquiry is a tool that points you directly back to your own being, to experience before the mind. If you read this book with your mind only, you are wasting your time. But if you read it with your whole being—if you listen to it, feel it, sense it, resonate with it, and digest it slowly, you may find that it is worthwhile after all.

I am not speaking to who you think you are. I am speaking to You, the Awareness behind the mask called "me." This book is for You. You will see your Self celebrated on every page.

—Adyashanti

WHO ARE YOU?

You Are . . .
beyond the body-mind and personality,
beyond all experience and the experiencer thereof,
beyond the world and its perceiver,
beyond existence and its absence,
beyond all assertions and denials.

Be still and awaken to the realization of who you Are.

In this realization of no separate self,
the Supreme Reality which you Are shines unobscured
in all things, as all things, and beyond all things.

Having returned to the formless Source
and transcended all separateness,
do not stop or cling even to this Source,
but go beyond to the Supreme Realization
which transcends all dualities,
yet does not deny even a speck of dust.

∽ CONTINUED ∽

The enlightened sage abides
as the eternal witness,
wholly unconcerned, yet intimately engaged.
Resting beyond all definitions,
he neither clings to transcendent freedom,
nor is he entangled by the dualistic world;
therefore, he is at one with all of life.

Living in the perfect trust of Supreme Realization,
he has nothing to gain or lose
and naturally manifests love, wisdom, and compassion—
without any personal sense of being the doer of deeds.

Having abandoned all concepts and ideas,
the enlightened sage lives as ever-present consciousness,
manifested and manifesting in the world of time and space
That which is eternal, ever new, and whole.

In this unobscured realization,
Supreme Reality shines Consciously
in all things, as all things, and beyond all things.
Shining unobscured, it penetrates the entire universe.
Penetrating the entire universe,
it knows itself as SELF.

One

THE EVOLUTIONARY IMPULSE TO BE FREE

Do not seek after what you yearn for,
seek the source of the yearning itself.

The impulse to be free is an evolutionary spark within consciousness which originates from beyond the ego. It is an impulse toward the divine, unity, and wholeness. It is an impulse originating from the Truth itself. This impulse to evolve is often co-opted by the ego, which then creates the illusion of the spiritual seeker. This impulse, which is inherently innocent, is something that, in and of itself, has nothing to do with any seeking to attain. It is only when the ego co-opts the impulse and then tries to attain something, that the seeker is born. This impulse, this spark of evolution, becomes almost instantly corrupted by a wanting which gives birth to the seeker.

Q: So then how does one not move away from that impulse, into striving and seeking? How do you stay in the impulse?

A: You stay in the impulse by seeing it as an impulse and not interpreting it as coming from a lack. A sense of lack is the ego's *interpretation* of the impulse which instantly gives rise to the separate, lost seeker. The impulse is an inner pressure to evolve, to become whole, to be free. It comes from your true nature, your already present divinity.

Q: So the pressure to evolve is interpreted as a lack.

A: Yes. Actually the impulse comes not from a lack, but from the spark of evolution. In that sense it comes from fullness. It comes from that which already is. The impulse to be free is actually coming directly from a freedom that is already starting to break into consciousness. The evolution is going from misunderstanding, which is ignorance, to Wisdom, which is Self realization. The impulse to be free comes from Wisdom.

Q: It seems so arrogant to think that I could be enlightened. I'm afraid to even entertain that possibility for fear that I'll just be disappointed. How could I be worthy of enlightenment?

A: The great good news is that you don't have to be worthy of enlightenment. Nobody's worthy of it. Despite unworthiness, it is given. Enlightenment is too big to be worthy of. Who could be worthy of it? Who is separate from it to be worthy? That's the Love. Worthiness doesn't count. Nothing can ostracize you from the Truth of your Self.

You have to allow yourself to be humbled. That humbling can take place in an instant or over a lifetime; it doesn't matter. Finally, when you become humble enough to come back to being nothing and to discovering your perfect nothingness, you discover everything. When that is discovered, it's important to be true to that and to not shrink away from it by saying, "Not me, no. It couldn't be me."

Q: I would like clarification. Isn't the spiritual seeker just an innocent expression of the impulse to be free?

A: It starts out as an innocent seeking, curiosity, or yearning, then the ego quickly corrupts it into a form of seeking for something outside of oneself. This is the birth of the seeker. There is only seeking without a seeker. Ask yourself: From where does the impulse, the yearning to be free, arise? Go to its source, to the fullness before all yearning.

Q: Is this seeking, which seems to be the natural outpouring of the impulse to be free, predestined and for the very few?

A: The impulse to be free is predestined in the sense that it does not originate in the ego. It is non-personal. When I say that the impulse is non-personal, I mean that it has nothing to do with you as a separate entity. In that sense it could be called predestined. But destiny is just another concept created by the ego, which exists and operates in terms of time. So the only conclusions that the ego can make will have to do with time. Both predestined and not predestined don't even exist outside the ego because when you are outside the ego, you are outside of time. The impulse to be free is not for the few. Many are called, few respond.

Q: What's the best thing I can do for my awakening?

A: Be with an enlightened teacher and listen. What I mean by that is, don't concern yourself with your mind's interpretation of the words. Just let the words in, without thinking about them or trying to understand them. Then they can penetrate to a place that is beyond the mind, and instead of your mind hearing them, your Self hears them. Doing this elicits what the words are meant to elicit—the Self. If you're not running the words through the mind, they go beyond the ego to Silence, to the Heart.

You are not a mistake or a problem to be solved.
Simply see your Self in its true light.

Q: To whom does the impulse to be free occur?

A: The impulse to be free is simply an arising within consciousness, which means it is not arising to anything. That's the whole point. Usually when the impulse to be free arises, the assumption is that it arose to a "me" who is in bondage. Outside of thought, there is no separate me and no bondage, only freedom.

Q: Is the me, the body-mind mechanism, necessary for freedom to come to fruition? Does it come to fruition?

A: Freedom comes to fruition when identification with the body-mind ceases. That is the fruition.

Q: If freedom is the end of identification with a conceptual me, will the impulse to be free have to be given up by the me?

A: No. What is given up is the me. The impulse to be free is non-personal, it can't be given up or clung to. Go backward to the source of the impulse to be free. This will take you beyond the me.

Q: Could the ego's apparent grasping at the impulse impede in any way the annihilation of the me?

A: Yes. It's the ego that in most seekers almost instantly corrupts the impulse. As soon as the impulse to be free is corrupted, the seeker is born. In most people this is inevitable; there is no blame assigned.

Q: The corruption is the ego saying, "This is mine; this is me," and making it personal. Is that correct?

A: Yes. It is important to keep in mind that when we say a powerful word like "corruption," we mean nothing more than "an innocent misunderstanding." Corruption in this sense is simply the expression of ignorance. It is innocent misunderstanding. Don't take the ego's antics as personal. You are not the ego. You are the consciousness of the ego.

Enlightenment depends to a large extent on believing that you are born for Freedom in this lifetime, and that it is available now, in this moment. The mind, which creates the past and future, keeps you out of the moment where the Truth of your Being can be discovered. In this moment, there is always Freedom and there is always peace. This moment in which you experience Stillness is every moment. Don't let the mind seduce you into the past or future. Stay in the moment, and dare to consider that you can be free now.

Q: This question has to do with choice. It seems like there really is no choice until there is some awakeness in the dream.

A: To think that I have choice or to state that I have no choice are both simply concepts in the mind completely devoid of any reality. The truth cannot be held within any concepts.

Q: Does the Impulse to be free have any boundaries?

A: No. There is no boundary to the impulse. The impulse comes from the infinite. If you have the impulse to be free, to be enlightened, to know God, then the timeless has already broken into this dream called me, to some extent.

Q: So boundaries are just another concept.

A: Yes. Concepts create boundaries. Concepts are boundaries, and they hem you in everywhere. Any concepts that the mind holds—like free will and destiny, choice and choicelessness, ego and the Self—create boundaries, limitations, prisons, and illusions.

Q: Is there any positive side of ego in this whole process?

A: Ego is neither positive nor negative. Those are simply concepts that create more boundaries. Ego is just ego, and the disaster of it all is that you, as a spiritual seeker, have been conditioned to think of the ego as bad, as an enemy, as something to be destroyed. This simply strengthens the ego. In fact, such conclusions arise from the ego itself. Pay no attention to them. Don't go to war with yourself; simply inquire into who you are.

~

What always is, is so easy to overlook because
it's not a thing and it's not an experience.

~

Q: How do you know if an impulse is a true impulse for freedom or just some other impulse?

A: Every human being on the face of this planet simply wants to be happy. The spiritual yogi and the strung-out drug addict both want to be happy. One of them is going about it in a wise way and the other in an ignorant way, but the impulse is the same.

When the impulse to be happy or free is immature, it takes the form of addictions of all sorts, desires of all sorts, indulgences of all sorts. But when the impulse is mature, it stops taking those forms, and there is no longer a moving away from anything. When one realizes that all the ways I have ever tried to be happy and all the ways I've tried to be free have not worked—at the moment that is seen, the impulse has shifted from something very immature to something mature.

Q: In that light, once one has become mature, doesn't that impulse automatically become fixed or stuck in wanting to be free?

A: Once the impulse is truly mature, one is no longer dominated by wanting—even spiritual wanting.

The whole point is to arrive at the place where the impulse or the yearning to be free is no longer driving you at all. This means that the impulse has accomplished its task—it has come to fulfillment, quietness, stillness, cessation. Even when this impulse has accomplished a good part of its task, very often the ego will cling to it as a distorted means of saving itself. So in the end, the impulse must be allowed to come to fruition. Fruition means that we have died into it. There is nothing for it to push anymore because we have *become* that impulse, that spark, that one Self.

Q: Does this yearning which takes you outward toward objects have a point at which it shifts to a yearning that takes you inward?

A: Yes. It shifts, but ultimately you don't even want to go inward. You want to be stopped in your tracks by the impulse. That is the whole point of the impulse: to be stopped dead in your tracks. To be stopped dead is to find the Self, God, the Infinite.

Two

INSECURITY AND THE UNKNOWN

*The door to God is
the insecurity of not knowing anything.
Bear the grace of that insecurity,
and all wisdom will be yours.*

Inherent in the impulse to be free, is insecurity. The impulse to be free comes from outside of the mind, and because of this, it makes the mind feel very insecure. Most spiritual seekers move away from this insecurity by seeking and striving for a distant spiritual goal. That's how they avoid feeling insecure. In an effort not to feel insecure, in an attempt not to directly face the Unknown—which is where the impulse to be free originates—the ego creates a spiritual seeker as a means to avoid it. It is a very intelligent play of the mind, a show, a fantasy.

Q: It's almost like a contradiction.

A: The impulse to be free, since it comes from outside of the mind, outside of the "me," is completely unknown to the mind, to the me. So the way the mind deals with this vast Unknown and this insecurity is by seeking. For many people, the impulse to be free simply solidifies the sense of a separate self rather than taking them beyond it. Seeking happens, but the seeker who is separate from the sought is purely a creation of the mind. You are not the seeker; you are the sought. You are the Self.

Q: Is the illusion of the seeker simply a disguised form of resistance to the impulse to be free?

A: Yes. Do not seek outside of yourself; you are the sought. Be still and all will come to you.

Q: If there was no resistance to it, would we stay receptive to the impulse to be free?

A: The whole point is receptivity to the impulse to be free. The impulse is like a seed that consciousness puts in the me, and all you have to do is be receptive to the seed. This means that in the presence of the impulse to be free, the truest most mature response would be simply to stop, be still, rest, and be taken. It is only the seeker that has absolutely no interest in stopping, but you are not the seeker.

You have to become more interested in the silent background than in the foreground, the phenomena: thoughts, emotions, sounds, smells, etc. Most people are focused on the foreground and what their five senses bring them, but the Self is discovered in the background. The Self is the source from which the phenomena spring and the ground in which this display of phenomena is happening, from the subtlest feelings and experiences to the grossest matter. When you rest as this background, you can taste your Self. You just give yourself to it. Actually, you're giving your *idea* of yourself to your true Self. The idea comes out of the Silence, so you give the idea of who you are back to Silence.

Q: I am interested in the seeking prior to the solidification of the seeker. It seems natural to move away from the overwhelming bodily sensation initiated by the impulse to be free . . . like when heat gets too hot, we move away. It also seems that the impulse has an inherent desire to move us or perhaps evolve in us or through us. How do you reconcile that natural tendency toward movement with the need to be still in the face of the impulse?

A: What needs to be seen is that for the impulse towards freedom to come to fruition, what you need to do is to jump into that heat. Jump into that fire. Do not give in to any tendency to move away. If you want to be cooked, you have to stay in the oven, in the fire of the impulse to be free.

Q: For many of us there have been periods of intense or prolonged fear. On my part it's been fear of not existing or not being. This fear seems to have arisen with what might be called "looking into the Unknown." How might one hold the Unknown until one sees that That is what we are?

A: Inquire into "Who is looking?" Is the one looking any different than the emptiness itself?

Q: No. Actually, no.

A: So in this recognition, what happens to the fear?

Q: It's gone.

Q: Since the Unknown stimulates a human being to feel insecure, how does anyone avoid this trap of the insecurity of the Unknown?

A: The insecurity of the Unknown is the very thing that you don't want to avoid. Within the insecurity, within the Unknown—the Mystery—lies the fulfillment of all seeking. Not until you come to absolute rest in that insecurity, in the Unknown, will it show its true face . . . which is beauty itself, beyond all fear. Total security arises out of total insecurity. Both security and insecurity refer to a personal, separate sense of I. Who is this I? In the absence of the personal I, all fears cease.

Q: When I look for myself inside the insecurity, there's absolutely nothing there.

A: But there *is* something there. Consciousness-ing is there. Awareness is there. That which has no image is there. That which is timeless is there. Eternal being-ness is there. Love is there. It is only the mind that looks into emptiness and says, "Nothing's there." What that really means is, there is no individual "I" there.

Q: That's what I was looking for.

A: (Laugh.) That's right. And the not finding of the I *is* freedom. It shows you just how much interest the mind has in anything other than itself: none! (Laugh.) It shows you just what the mind is focused on.

Q: Can you talk about the fear of the Unknown, about the frustration of not getting there quickly enough?

A: Frustration comes from wanting, anticipating, hoping. What is it that you are anticipating?

Q: Shedding all the shackles.

A: There are no shackles to be shed. They are all concepts, all ideas, all beliefs that you've been taught.

Q: So once you realize they're all concepts, you've just jumped off the cliff?

A: Yes. If you've truly realized that, then the jumping has already happened. It's over.

Realization is different than knowledge. Knowledge won't get you anywhere. Realization is spontaneous and intuitive. Leave all knowledge behind. Let yourself not know anything, and fall awake.

Q: In not-knowing, there doesn't seem to be a lot of wisdom of love. At least it's not obvious. What I see more is the impurity.

A: Then you're not in not-knowing. You're in judgment, which means you're in the known. You're in the mind, which is interpreting your experience.

Q: I think you're right, and I want to clarify. What I see is the corruption of the ego. It's seen over and over.

A: The seeing is outside of what's being seen. That's where the wisdom lies: in the seeing itself, in the awareness itself, and in the consciousness of what's happening. That's where the wisdom is.

The mind will always want to remain fixated on the content of perception. But wisdom arises from the consciousness of the content. So it's important to see that the content of perception *is* the dream, *is* unimportant, *is* illusion.

Q: What's missing is the realization that it is illusion or that it is a dream. It still seems very real most of the time—maybe all the time.

A: So take the story, "What's missing is the realization that this is illusion," and discard it. What's left?

Q: There's just awareness.

A: You are That.

Q: You rarely speak about God. What is God to you?

A: In order to find what the concept of God is pointing to, you must let go of your image of God and every concept you have about God. You must dare to be void of all concepts and enter into perfect Emptiness, perfect stillness, and perfect silence. You must forget everything you have ever learned about God. It won't help you. It may comfort you, but such comfort is imaginary; it is an illusion. Let go of all the false comforts of the mind. Let them all come to an end. The end must be experienced fully in Stillness. When you let all images, all concepts, all hopes, and all beliefs end, Stillness is experienced.

Experience the core of Stillness. Dive into it and surrender fully. In full surrender to Stillness, you directly experience That to which the concept of God points. In that direct experience, you awaken from the dream of the mind and realize that the concept of God points to who you truly are.

If you choose Freedom, life will become magical. The life you'll step into is one in which the Self is in hidden agreement with your humanness. The Self begins to harmonize with your life, and it may proceed in a way that you could never have predicted. The magical part is that the more you let go, the better it feels. The more you step into insecurity, the more you notice how secure and safe it is. Where you just stepped *out of* was unsafe. Everyone is so miserable because they seek security in things that are limited and always moving and changing unpredictably.

Three

MEDITATION AND SPIRITUAL PRACTICES

*When you cease trying
to control and manipulate your experience,
meditation spontaneously happens.*

True meditation has no direction, goals, or method. All methods aim at achieving a certain state of mind. All states are limited, impermanent, and conditioned. Fascination with states leads only to bondage and dependency. True meditation is abidance as primordial consciousness.

True meditation appears in consciousness spontaneously when awareness is not fixated on objects of perception. When you first start to meditate you notice that awareness is always focused on objects: on thoughts, bodily sensations, emotions, memories, sounds, etc. This is because the mind is conditioned to focus and contract upon objects. Then the mind compulsively interprets what it is aware of (the object) in a mechanical and distorted way. It begins to draw conclusions and make assumptions according to past conditioning.

In true meditation, all objects are left to their natural functioning. This means that no effort should be made to manipulate or suppress any object of awareness. In true meditation, the emphasis is on being awareness; not on being aware of objects, but on resting as primordial awareness itself. Primordial awareness, consciousness, is the source in which all objects arise and subside. As you gently relax into awareness, into listening, the mind's compulsive contraction around objects will fade. Silence of being will come more clearly into your consciousness, welcoming you to rest and abide. An attitude of open receptivity, free of any goal or anticipation, will facilitate the presence of silence and stillness, and reveal them to be your natural condition.

Silence, stillness, and awareness are not states and therefore cannot be produced or created. Silence is the non-state in which all states arise and subside. Silence is itself the eternal witness without form or attribute. As you rest more profoundly as the witness, all objects take on their natural functionality, and awareness becomes free of the mind's compulsive contractions and identifications, and returns to its natural non-state of Presence.

The simple yet profound question "Who Am I?" can then reveal one's self not to be the endless tyranny of the ego-personality, but objectless Freedom of Being—the Primordial Consciousness in which all states and all objects come and go as manifestations of the eternal unborn Self that YOU ARE.

Q: What is the purpose of meditation?

A: The purpose of meditation is to find the meditator. When you look for the meditator, you won't find him, her, or it. All you'll find is silent Emptiness. In finding Emptiness, the mind stops. If you let it, Emptiness will stop the mind—unless you run back into samsara, into the mind's drama of thinking, striving, and confusion. When you allow Emptiness to stop your mind, you'll awaken and realize that you are that Emptiness. You'll realize that you are not the mind or the body or any meditative phenomena.

You are Emptiness. Emptiness means limitless, boundless, Pure Consciousness.

You are not a thing. You are not a body-thing or a mental-thing or an emotional-thing or a thing with a history in time. You are no-thing. You are Consciousness itself. Let go of your attachment to thing-ness, and you will awaken to that which is the Source of all things. You are that Source. Go directly to that Source. Don't waste your lifetime defining yourself as a thing. Wake up from that dream, and you are Free.

Your thoughts, concepts, ideas, and imaginings cannot touch Truth. There is nothing you can do to awaken to it. Absolutely nothing. When you realize that there is nothing you can do, that all doing will only lead you further away from it, you must stop all doing. Stop and be still. Stopping and stillness require no doing and no effort.

All of your life you have been taught to do, to strive, to effort. You have been sold a self-improvement plan. You have been conditioned to believe that you are the body and the mind. All of this is a reflection of ignorance. It has been the blind leading the blind.

The truth of your being is Openness. It needs no practice, technique or manipulation to realize. Who you are is free, now! Who you are will not become free or liberated at some point in the future; who you are is Liberated, now! Stop all doing and be still. Let the fire of stillness burn everything and reveal That which is Openness.

Q: What is renunciation?

A: Anyone can renounce things, people, places, or lifestyles. But only a true renunciate renounces interest in his own mind—renounces his ideas, his beliefs, his hopes, his conditioning, his wounds, his defeats, his victories, his past, and his future.

Many clothe themselves in the robes of false renunciation, but true renunciates are very rare, and very free.

Concentration techniques assume that Awareness isn't present and therefore must be found. The problem with these techniques is that they leave you thinking you have to do something to manufacture Awareness, when it's actually present in everyone all the time. Awareness is something that already is, so there's nothing we need to do to get it. The deeper the relaxation, the more obvious it is that you are this Aware Space.

Abiding means letting everything be as it already is—no matter what it is. If you're feeling good, let that be as it is. If you're feeling bad, let that be as it is. No matter what your emotional, physical, or mental state, let it be as it is and don't wish it to be otherwise. If you want it to be different from what it is, you're not abiding; you're picking and choosing and trying to control your experience.

Q: How different are your techniques from what Buddha taught?

A: I don't think in terms of having or using techniques. Any technique that is used mechanically tends to condition the mind further. Our natural condition is one of peace and stillness. Who is interested in techniques? Only the mind. All techniques are for the mind, but you are not the mind. Direct insight and experience reveal your Self to be Freedom. You don't need techniques to be as you truly are. Simply be still. But don't try to be still. Make no effort, and stillness comes to you. Let go of all concepts, ideas, beliefs, identities, hopes, pasts, and futures. You've been told that this is difficult and that you need techniques, but this is only a thought—the blind leading the blind. Throw this thought away and see what you find.

Q: Staying in the Stillness is very hard because the mind starts and traps me again. I just passed this gateless gate and realized that there wasn't a gate, but now I see the gate again!

A: You see the *appearance* of a gate, the illusion of a gate. Now the experience is very different because you know the gate is only an appearance—it's not real. It's like a mirage, an illusion. Before, you didn't know that; you thought the gate was real. You banged on it and rattled its doors, trying to open this gate of awakening.

Q: Now I'm oscillating between Emptiness and the concept of who I am, and this causes suffering.

A: Emptiness feels free and liberating and serene, and the concept of "I" feels like a tight fist. The oscillating from I am free to I am bound is a beautiful opportunity to look afresh at your experience and inquire anew: What doesn't come and go? This leads to a deeper awakening, a deeper experience of what doesn't come and go. All experience comes and goes, no matter how sublime, but the *source* of these experiences, the Awareness, doesn't come and go.

By going nowhere, continue to experience having arrived. By not taking one step in any direction, you arrive instantly. You arrive by not going anywhere. Just stay there. Just see that you are always That, even if the mind creates a story line telling you that you are other than That.

Most people fret about losing this state or that state. They get caught up in what's not present anymore. That which comes and goes is not real; quit chasing it. It doesn't matter. What *haven't* you lost? That is what's important. What always is? What is there in bliss and in misery? Who you are is always present and is always the same. That which doesn't come and go is real. That is where Freedom is found—nowhere else.

It doesn't matter how profound a vision is or how wonderful the kriyas, or the kundalini, or the bliss. No matter how beautiful the spiritual experience is, it is only an experience, and experiences come and go. Freedom is found only in that which does not come and go. If it doesn't come and go, that means that it's present *now*. When you have a beautiful spiritual experience and then seem to lose it, ask yourself: What was present then that is still present now? Then, you know where to put all of your attention, all of your dedication, and all of your heart. Don't put it anywhere else. You are that permanence which contains all becoming and all be-going.

Q: It seems like the clarity of who I am comes and goes.

A: The key word is "seems." Does it really come and go?

Q: No.

A: If you put all of your spiritual eggs in that basket—in that one truth—and dedicate everything to that and that alone, if you let the recognition of that deepen and deepen, you will discover a freedom that will spin your head right off your shoulders.

Q: How does one eliminate feelings, thoughts, grief, fear, or cravings, and addictions while meditating? Are positive affirmations useful for this?

A: Stop trying to eliminate anything. It is the belief that a thing needs to be eliminated that maintains its existence. Be an open space for whatever arises. Notice that you are the space in which everything arises. When everything is allowed to arise, you have the opportunity to perceive That which does not arise or subside. You Are That.

Positive affirmations are for the mind only. Leave the mind to the mind. You are not this mind. Stop trying to rearrange your mind and discover what lies before it. You are the consciousness that contains the mind. Ask yourself this question, before the mind, body and emotions: Who am I? Meditate on that. Seek the Seeker.

The aim of spiritual practice is to discover in your own present experience That which the movement of thought never touches. This does not mean to suppress the thinking mind, nor does it mean to attempt to understand by using thought. What I am pointing toward is the Unknown: the already, ever-present, silent, still source that not only proceeds thought but surrounds it. You must become more interested in the Unknown than in that which is known. Otherwise, you will remain enslaved by the very narrow and distorted perspective of conceptual thinking. You must go so deeply into the Unknown that you are no longer referencing thought to tell you who and what you are. Only then will thought be capable of reflecting that which is true, rather than falsely masquer-ading as truth.

What I am talking about is a condition where the mind never fixates, where it never closes, where it has no compulsive need to understand in terms of ideas, concepts, and beliefs. A condition where you are no longer referencing the mind, feeling, or emotions for security in any way. What I am talking about is the complete surrender of all separateness until liberation becomes a permanent condition, and you are forever lost in the freedom of the Absolute.

Four

MOVING BEYOND
THE IMPULSE TO STRUGGLE

*Realization is the medicine given
to the disease of suffering—
and it's the only medicine there is.*

The most challenging thing for the spiritual seeker to do is to stop struggling. The human condition is characterized by a constant state of struggle which manifests as conflict, fear, and confusion. These various states of tension, caused by the compulsive and mechanical impulse to struggle, distort our ability to perceive what is true and liberating. What is truly interesting is that the human condition contains within it an unconscious need to struggle. Why? Because by remaining in a state of constant struggle we maintain the boundaries that create the sense of a separate self, a self who unconsciously defines itself as "the one who struggles." And even more shocking is the discovery that not only do we need to struggle in order to remain separate, but we *want* to remain separate—even though it causes so much suffering, fear, and confusion. We want to remain separate because by remaining separate we maintain the sense of being someone different, special, and unique.

Many people are addicted to, and identified with, being the separate and unique victims of the tragic dramas of their lives. People so often form the deepest bonds with one another by sharing the painful and tragic episodes of their lives, as if those episodes define who they really are. Many people really see themselves as "the one who has struggled," and "the one who is struggling now." Others struggle to hold onto a more positive, fixed identity as a good, successful, or spiritual person. However, most people cling to both negative and positive self images, creating an endless struggle between contradictory identities that have no fundamental reality to begin with. Is it any wonder that so many spiritual seekers remain so confused?

The most insidious and unconscious way that spiritual seekers struggle is by struggling with practices and techniques that are supposed to help them stop struggling. But who has the biggest investment in these practices? The sense of a separate self, or ego, does. Only the ego asks how to stop struggling because all how-to questions lead to further struggle. This mechanism of maintaining struggle is how the ego maintains control. Struggling only ceases when you passionately inquire into who and what you truly *are*— deeply enough to awaken from the dream of being a personal, separate self.

Again, the reason that you struggle is in order to maintain a sense of a separate self, a self which is ultimately nothing more than a defense mechanism against the revelation that no separate self actually exists. As soon as you stop struggling, you lose the boundaries that give you the sense of a separate self. With nothing to oppose, the false sense of self evaporates into nothingness, into the Unknown, and you suddenly feel very lost with no familiar ground to stand on. Your identity is cut loose from all that is familiar and known, and you find yourself floating in a vast expanse with nothing to grab hold of. This groundless expanse is the foretaste of liberation, but few choose to remain in this unknown territory. Instead, most people begin to struggle in opposition to the unknown and unfamiliar vastness until they, once again, begin to feel secure in a familiar sense of self and separation. Faced with a freedom that is absolute, a freedom that leaves no room for separation from the whole, most people will compulsively contract back into a condition of struggle where they can maintain a familiar sense of self. This means that when actually given the choice, most people will choose to struggle and remain separate, rather than to face the austerity of a freedom that shatters any sense of separateness. It is only when you desire to be free more than you desire the security of a familiar sense of self that you spontaneously move into a freedom that is final and beyond struggle.

Habitually conditioned to avoid fear and insecurity, most people compulsively cling to what is familiar, even if it is very painful and confusing. I have witnessed countless people turn away from the experience and revelation of freedom because in that freedom there is nowhere to hide and nothing to hold onto. As they begin to awaken to a freedom that is profound, many turn back to a familiar condition of struggle and confusion in an unconscious effort to avoid stepping completely into the ungraspable and indefinable mystery of liberation. Why? Because in that mystery there is absolutely nothing for the personal ego to attain or define itself by.

This is not the liberation that most people envision when they start out. Consciously or unconsciously most people envision a freedom that they can attain and possess. So many who glimpse the enlightened condition tell me that it is so much bigger than they ever could have imagined. To realize that freedom is not something that you possess, but something that possesses you, is often experienced as shocking, frightening, and unbelievably liberating. It is a revelation that swallows up the dream of a separate you and reveals Self to be a limitless expanse. What I am describing is the experience of Self void of any sense of selfhood, a timeless and uncaused condition which is constantly birthing manifest existence into form.

To have a glimpse of this profound freedom requires very little, but to *live* it requires the destruction of every concept of self you have ever held or will ever hold. This freedom is a flame that burns the need to struggle to ash and reveals one's Self to be all that is.

Q: I've been experiencing being really open, followed by being contracted when there's egoic wanting. It seems that I don't really want to give up the egoic wanting.

A: Is that true?

Q: No.

A: So what do you get out of telling yourself that story?

Q: I get to focus on me.

A: Do you like to focus on me?

Q: No. Not really. It's not satisfying. It's experiencing confusion, separateness, wanting.

A: So what is satisfying, truly satisfying?

Q: To tell the truth.

A: And what is the truth? . . . What is the truth you truly want, yearn for, desire to tell yourself?

Q: I'm not sure. Or maybe I just don't know, or am overlooking it.

A: Find that out.

Five

CEASING TO BECOME

There's nothing to do, nothing to be,
and nothing to become.
There's nowhere to go and no experience to have.

Ceasing to become means that in the face of that which the mind can never know, you do not move. As long as you are trying to become, trying to get somewhere, trying to attain something, you are quite literally moving away from the Truth itself. In order to cease becoming, you must reject the path and the journey. You must reject time, which means the future, which means that tomorrow is never going to come. Enlightenment will never happen tomorrow. Tomorrow is becoming, and becoming is time, and time is thought. Thought is the garbage can. If you look into the garbage can, all you will get is garbage.

To rest in the Unknown literally means that your mind knows absolutely nothing about how to get you to your goal. It means that you've stopped looking toward the mind to tell you how, when, and where. By absolutely ceasing to become, you stop. This stopping is effortless. It comes out of wisdom.

Q: There seems to be a doing-ness in ceasing. How does one cease the doing-ness of becoming? How does one do that?

A: Seeing, perceiving, that there is nothing that you can do to cease anything—that itself brings the ceasing. As long as there is a belief that *you* can do the ceasing, then ceasing will never happen. Only when it's perceived that the you who is trying to cease is just a thought, and therefore an illusion, does ceasing happen spontaneously.

To be lost in not knowing is a wonderful place to be. When you're lost in not knowing, you come to know, but not in the way that you knew before. You come to know as a moment-to-moment experience of being. That's your knowing. And you know that That is who you really are. You *are* that ever-unfolding mystery beyond the mind.

Q: I feel the drive to seek. I feel it at a physical level.

A: The drive is reflected in the physical body, but where does that drive originate? Where does that sensation in the body originate?

Q: There's an anxiety.

A: Where does it come from? Where does the sensation come from?

Q: It doesn't come from anywhere.

A: Ah!

Q: It's just there.

A: That nowhere-ness, that emptiness, is before body, before mind, the source of all. Stop, now. For once in your life, just stop. No thinking. Just stop.

Go to the pure I AM. Not I am *this* or I am *that*, but simply I AM. Then throw out the I, so that there is only AM. This is the stateless state, the ultimate principle, the absolute Self. Everything, in essence, is this absolute principle called the Self.

❁

Q: Is the self-revealing discovery that there is no one to do the seeking or to cease seeking, the end of becoming?

A: Yes. You know that has happened when the dream called "me" has stopped holding any importance or significance whatsoever. When you realize that the individual me is completely insignificant, this is the fulfillment of the seeking, the realization of no seeker. You realize that it is all a dream of consciousness. This could be called the direct path, where the seeker is never allowed to take the first step.

Q: What do we call that point at which we let go of the seeker?

A: Death.

Q: And what is death?

A: The cessation of the seeker.

❁

Q: I've heard it said that the ego must die in order to be enlightened. What does ego death mean?

A: It is said that the ego must die in order for you to truly live. But nothing need die, you simply need to grow up. A child does not die in order to grow into an adult. The child simply grows up; it evolves and leaves behind what is no longer appropriate. See that the ego is no longer useful or appropriate and leave it behind. Only the ego makes its own demise seem dramatic.

Questions that are pregnant with transformative power assert themselves in consciousness as something that you simply cannot avoid. Those are the questions that are worthwhile.

Q: Are questions simply a reflection of consciousness on a mind that is ready to be transformed?

A: The mind is never ready to be transformed. Transformation happens, that is all.

Q: If the Self is beyond becoming, what is it that becomes?

A: Nothing becomes. Thought and experience simply dance, giving the experience of becoming and be-going. But in truth, everything happens spontaneously and is uncaused.

Q: Then what is it that needs to cease becoming in order to find out who we are?

A: The idea that you, as a separate entity, are going to cease or not cease.

The problem is that most people are paying attention to objects, to what they perceive—rather than to the ultimate perceiver, the background. Either way, awareness is happening 100% of the time. The light is on brightly. It never goes off, but where is it looking? The human condition is characterized by a complete fascination with objects, starting with this object that we interpret as "me." Me is only a thought. You are before this me thought.

This life is a dream. To call it a dream is not to disparage it; that doesn't mean it isn't worthwhile. It's no different from dreams you have at night. You wake up from your dreams into this dream we call life, and when you go to sleep, you wake up in another dream world. But that which is awake in both worlds, the Dreamer, is always the same. Awareness is always present. *That's* the reality. What doesn't come and go, even in the dream-state? That's who you are.

Q: Is it true that there needs to be a letting go of the mis-identification with illusion or the dream in order to allow for Self realization? Is it just identification that's the malady, the problem?

A: All barriers are conceptual—made of ideas, beliefs, and opinions. Outside of concepts and beliefs, there is no barrier. Belief is what the mind does to fill up emptiness, to give it something to look at, to play with, to hide behind.

Q: So our conclusions, interpretations, concepts, and beliefs are the manifestation of conditioning.

A: Yes. Without concepts and beliefs, there is no conditioning. You have to have these to be a separate somebody.

Q: When we cease becoming, what do we find?

A: Peace, cessation, eternal Self. There is no longer struggle. You are free.

Q: How do I reconcile allowing things to be as they are with taking a stand? There are a lot of areas in my life where I feel I can't just allow things to be as they are, but I must take up arms and oppose them.

A: There's never a need to oppose. Opposition is an attitude of the separate self. Do what is true. In doing what is true, there is no attitude of opposition.

Q: It wouldn't feel right in my soul to lay back and do nothing. It would be cowardly. At times, allowing things to be as they are can enter into the realm of cowardice.

A: Let the Truth inform action.

Q: Does that kind of action come from a feeling about what's right under the circumstances?

A: It's before feeling.

Q: Even at the risk of consequences?

A: The Truth doesn't care about consequences. It's concerned with the Truth. It doesn't care if you're liked or not liked. You won't always be liked for it, and sometimes you will be disliked for it. As long as you're acting in the world based on what you like or don't like, or what others like or don't like, you're not in the realm of Truth. Truth insists that we not only be truthful, but that we act truthfully. It's not enough just to know the Truth. You have to *be* it—to act it, and to do it.

Many spiritual people are involved in a radical denial of what is happening. They want to transcend it, get rid of it, get out of it, get away from it. There's nothing wrong with that *feeling*, but the approach doesn't work because it's escapism in spiritual clothing. It's wearing spiritual clothing and spiritual concepts, but it is really no different than a drunk in the gutter who doesn't want to feel the pain anymore. When you abide and accept everything completely and fully, you automatically go beyond.

No beliefs and no concepts are true.
Throw them all out and let the flame of silence
burn you awake.

Q: I thought I made a commitment to Truth, but I still haven't found it.

A: As soon as you want the Truth more than anything else, you'll get it. That's how it works. It's pretty simple.

Q: Is making this choice something that happens over time?

A: If you want it to.

Q: Is this a choice that you just have to keep making?

A: You continue to choose this until you don't have to choose anymore.

Q: I want it so badly that I'll give up anything for it.

A: Are you willing to give up pretending that you don't already have it?

Q: Why don't more people become enlightened?

A: Because they are still finding entertainment in the dream to some extent.

Six

AWAKENING

You are the light of awareness—
the source and expression of all that is.

At the moment of enlightenment everything falls away— everything. Suddenly the ground beneath you is gone, and you are alone. You are alone because you have realized that there is no other; there is no separation. There is only you, only Self, only limitless Emptiness, pure Consciousness.

To the mind, the ego, this appears terrifying. When it looks at limitlessness and infinity, it sees meaninglessness and despair. However, the view changes to unending joy and wonder once the mind is let go of.

When you are enlightened, you stand alone. You need no supports of any kind because there is nothing to support; a separate you no longer exists. You realize that the whole ego experience was a flimsy illusion. You stand alone but are never, never lonely because everywhere you look, all you see is That, and You are That.

Q: Is awakening just another spiritual experience you have?

A: Awakening doesn't mean *you* awaken. It means that there is only awakening. There is no "you" who is awake, there is only awakeness. As long as you identify with a "you" who is either awake or not awake, you are still dreaming. Awakening is awakening from the dream of a separate you into simply being Awakeness.

Q: When a person becomes awake and enlightened does he or she also become wise and loving?

A: When you awaken, all becoming ceases. Being awake means that you realize by direct experience who and what you are. You do not become anything. All becoming is in time, which is mind. Awakening is outside of time: You awaken from time to That which is timeless. Wisdom and love are aspects of your own Self and as such do not need to be created or pursued.

Many people *try* to become wiser and more loving, and they remain in a constant battle with themselves. This approach never works because it assumes a separate "you" who wants to be a better person. It is the you that is the dream, a thought only. In taking yourself to be a separate entity, you blind yourself to the truth of your being, which *is* Love and Wisdom.

Q: I have moments when it seems as though I've gained enlightenment. Then, after some time, that state disappears. Does the time come when you don't lose it?

A: The word "enlightenment" points to who you are. Who you are is not a state that can be gained or lost. It is not a spiritual experience. All states and experiences come and go. Who you are is the permanence existing right now, regardless of states and experiences.

In one sense, the enlightened life is one of total insecurity; you live and act from the Unknown. We're used to acting from the distorted sense of security that our mind provides, but Freedom doesn't operate that way. It's a paradox. Precisely because you don't know, and you know you don't know, the door is wide open to know in each moment. That's when you know—in each moment. By resting in not knowing, knowing becomes available.

Looking inside yourself
and not finding yourself
is the finding!

When fascination with the me dissolves, when it simply no longer holds center stage in your awareness, then all that remains in the absence of the me, is revealed.

When fascination with the me dissolves, when it simply no longer holds center stage in your awareness, then all that remains in the absence of the me, is revealed.

The person whose realization is profound has become the evolutionary force of consciousness. They've become that. And the evolutionary force of consciousness to awaken is only concerned with the truth.

Seven

EMBODIMENT: TRUE NON-DUALITY

First you awaken out of life, then you awaken as Life itself.

After sudden Awakening to the Self, there begins a process of gradual embodiment of the transcendent into the human personality. By gradual I mean the deepening of realization after the experience of enlightenment. The more the transcendent Self becomes embodied within our humanness, the more vast our view becomes, and the more we express and manifest transcendent realization in the way we live life.

This process of embodiment is a continual stripping away of every remnant of attachment and ego. It is a movement of continual surrender to the vast implications contained within true spiritual Awakening. It is a phase of spiritual unfolding fraught with many dangers, self-deceptions, and misunderstandings. It is where many seekers of liberation succumb to fear, doubt, and a lack of conviction. The process of embodiment can be simultaneously very thrilling and quite disorienting. It is an area of incredible subtlety and complexity which few truly understand.

Q: When I hear the term "embody" the first image that my mind comes up with is some great vastness that I'm somehow going to bring into this physical form. Yet we speak of embodiment occurring only when there is no longer a somebody. Can you speak about what the body is, in the teaching of embodiment?

A: Embodiment starts with the realization that every manifest thing and non-thing constitutes your true body. Your humanness is simply a reflection of the depth of your realization. So it's not that you have to do something to the human body to make it a bigger, vaster, or wider container for the truth of being to come through. What's most important is to perceive your *entire* body, which is everything. Then, your humanness will reflect the depth of that realization. Embodiment is not something that you do; it is something that is a result of how far you take enlightenment and how much of yourself you give to it. The entire cosmos is your body. Let your humanness reflect and manifest the whole.

Q: So, embodiment is not about bringing the vastness into me; it's about giving myself to the vastness.

A: Yes. This is the correct understanding.

Q: Is embodiment possible if the identification with a "me" is at all present? If not, what are the indications of embodiment?

A: Embodiment is usually a gradual process that begins after the event called "awakening," so we can't really speak about embodiment in absolute terms. The indications of embodiment are peace, love, wisdom, and enlightened action. What effect we have on others is a good indication of exactly how enlightened we are. If we think we are very enlightened, but have a negative effect on others, we are probably not nearly as enlightened as we'd like to believe. This is not to say that others will always like the way we behave, since enlightened behavior is often misunderstood by a mind still dwelling in separation. Enlightened behavior liberates. It doesn't matter if someone likes it or not, the question is, does it liberate? That's the only question worthwhile, and it's the only proof of enlightenment.

Enlightened action springs from a humility that never makes assumptions about one's own attainment. The more humble you are, the better chance that your behavior will be enlightened.

Q: Can you say a little more about what goes on with the body when the boundaries of the self dissolve?

A: As the opening begins and deepens, the body may go through a tremendous amount. Kundalini is usually said to be responsible for these events, but if we just call it the energy of the body, it's easier to talk about it.

As the opening progresses, the body must readjust. When space opens up, it provides room for the body to re-harmonize and to return to its natural state. During this process, some people's bodies experience a real shake-down. This can be quite dramatic because energy that has been trapped on the various levels—physical, mental, emotional, and spiritual—is released. This trapped energy is what keeps you off-balance and in a state of suffering. Suddenly all the tension, holding, and knots are released, and the energy goes out in all directions.

This energy has to break loose before it can re-harmonize and get into the proper flow. This bursting out can feel exhilarating or terrible; it can be tremendously powerful or mild. The harmonization may take weeks, months, or years. It may be very strong or imperceptible. Everyone is different; it just depends on how out-of-whack you've been.

Q: What is the most important element in opening the way to embodiment of the teaching?

A: Perceive the teaching as an expression of your own Self, then you won't see yourself as distant from it. Then it won't become a goal for you to obtain; it will be seen as a reflection of your own heart. Seeing it in this way orients you to the most effective attitude. If you see a spiritual teaching as a reflection of your own Self, your own depth, then your relationship with it is going to be far different than if you perceived the teaching as coming from other than yourself. It's the difference between teaching that leads to more isolation and separation, and teaching that leads to less isolation and separation. Your attitude is all-important.

Q: It seems that this attitude would negate the apparent problem of what to do with this "me."

A: The correct attitude toward the teaching negates the illusion of the me instantly. It's only when you think the teaching is coming from something other than your own Self, that it creates further separation. If you think the teaching is something other than a reflection of what you already know to be true in your heart, then it creates the illusion of me, the seeker.

Q: Can the mind actually hold this vastness of love full-time, or is it held in the heart?

A: I can't relate to the concept of holding. How can you hold what you are?

Q: I guess the mind doesn't understand how actions appear to come from that place where everything is one.

A: Don't look to the mind. Don't think; just be. Be still and know your Self. Before the movement of mind lies emptiness. Emptiness is the gateway of Heart Wisdom: the spontaneous, intuitive intelligence, which originates from the Self.

Having a profound awakening can be like taking the lid off of a jar. All the karma that has been repressed, all the karma at the bottom of our misery that we aren't conscious of, comes flying out because there is finally space in which it can emerge. When it hits you in the face, you wonder where your Freedom went and what went wrong. But understand that this is a consequence of the

Freedom; it is not a mistake. Everything wants to come up into and be transformed by the Freedom. If you let it come up into this Aware Space, which is Love, it will re-harmonize. This Space that you are is unconditional Love. Unconditional means just that: everything is welcome; nothing is cast away or set apart from it.

Q: My mind has the tendency to judge actions as coming from truth or not coming from truth, and yet I never seem to be sure what the truth actually is. How do I come to a place of knowingness of what the truth is in any given circumstance?

A: The mechanism of self-evaluation *is* what distorts the perception of truth. Knowingness of the truth arises from a silent mind, a mind that is not evaluating and struggling to know. The perception arises from resting in the Unknown, in not knowing. If you come to rest in not knowing, you will immediately know.

Q: But sometimes I rest in not knowing and still I never seem to come to know.

A: You must rest in not knowing with curiosity. Even though you rest in not knowing, you still need to remain curious. You still want to know, but you no longer struggle to know. Just observe and stay sensitive to the movement of knowingness within. Knowingness is experienced in your being as aliveness. It is not in your mind.

Listen from the neck down. Be in your being, and you will come to feel what I am speaking of within yourself.

Q: You've said that if we knew how much we impacted the whole we would be crushed. Would you speak about that in relationship to embodiment?

A: As long as the me is trying to contain the non-personal view of oneness, it's always going to feel crushed by it. The non-personal view is going to be too big for it; of course, that's the whole point. The revelation of oneness crushes the me when it's seen absolutely clearly, when it's seen that I am the One.

There is a big difference between perceiving oneness and perceiving that I *am* that One. Once you truly start to live in the revelation that I am the One, the embodiment of that revelation in and through the human being and human personality begins to happen. If the mind clings to separation, then that individual is going to find himself suffering far, far more than he did before he knew that everything is one.

Q: How do I integrate spirituality into my everyday life?

A: The question should not be "How to integrate?" It should be "Who is the integrator?" Once you go beyond the integrator, there is no longer the perception of a duality that needs to be integrated.

Integration is between two. There is no such distinction between everyday life and spirituality. Integration means that you are still holding onto the false distinctions of the mind. Cling neither to spiritual states nor mundane states. You are the stateless state. All is included within, and is, an expression of your Self. Throw out the concept of "spiritual" and throw out the concept of "everyday life." There is only Life, undivided and whole.

Q: How do I live and manifest in the relative world the truth that I know through deep spiritual experience?

A: Let your inner spiritual revelation become deep enough to include the whole world of time and space. If your spiritual revelation is only big enough to go *beyond* the relative world but not *include* it, then you will continue to experience a duality and therefore a struggle with the relative world. Do not become attached to the realm of the absolute. See the absolute and the relative as an undivided whole, as two expressions of the same supreme reality that you are. Go beyond all dualities to the source of duality, to that which is neither this nor that but expresses itself as this and that.

Q: Since human nature is always expressing itself throughout one's life as a personality, how does one know how much non-duality has been embodied within oneself?

A: As long as there is somebody reflecting back and measuring, then the dissolving is not complete. The most important dissolving is the dissolving of the mind's tendency to reference itself—in any way whatsoever. I'm talking about a willingness to die into the Unknown—which means no self-referencing.

Q: So then how is a life that is fully embodied in non-duality lived? What are its characteristics?

A: Wonder. You are always surprised. You are always, always, always surprised because there is no longer a clinging to past, present, or future.

The human being is what links consciousness to its own infinite expressions in form. Through the form of an awake human being, consciousness becomes conscious of itself as both formlessness and as all forms. This is why, to the true sage, everything is divine, whole, and complete. Everything is God, the Self.

Q: What is the difference between self-inquiry and self-referencing, and how does that relate to embodiment?

A: What I am speaking about in embodiment is a continuation of self-inquiry. For most people self-inquiry stops at the realization that I am formless consciousness. But when I am speaking of embodiment, I'm taking self-inquiry back into the world, the world which still remains whether it's perceived as a dream or not. This is an inquiry into what that world is.

The realization, "I am formless consciousness," is simply the opposite of "I am an individual somebody." Even with that realization, there is still going to remain the appearance of somebody. So embodiment is simply a reflection of the realization that every manifest thing that exists is the one body of the one consciousness. This is a return to wholeness, to a completeness that includes the un-manifest and the manifest alike. It is perceiving that both formless consciousness and the world of form are simply two aspects of an unnamable, mysterious whole.

Self-referencing is the mind's tendency to locate itself. Anything that you can perceive is partial, and therefore cannot contain your whole Self. So when it's realized that there is no self apart from the perceiving, then the tendency to try to find one's Self in any experience, insight, or concept—ceases. This is why the highest attainment is not an experience, and it is not something perceivable. It is the death of trying to find yourself because there is no self apart from consciousness.

There is only the perceiving, there's no body that perceives. When it is realized that there is no body perceiving and that perceiving is all there is, then quite naturally the perceiving and what is perceived are seen to be two aspects of a unified whole, like heads and tails on a coin. Heads and tails on a coin cannot be separated.

The body is a sensing instrument of consciousness. Without the body and the mind, the trees couldn't see themselves. Usually we think that we are looking at a tree, but the tree is looking at itself through us. Without this instrument, the tree doesn't get to see itself. We are sensing instruments of the Divine.

Q: How do you define non-duality?

A: Cessation of conceptualization. Perceiving before the mind. Perceiving without mind.

Enlightened action leaves no trace. Enlightened action comes directly from Emptiness, not from the mind. It is spontaneous. If it comes in the form of words, the words come from Emptiness. If it comes in the form of actions, the actions come from Emptiness—from *before* the personality and the mind.

Eight

A LOVE GREATER THAN ONESELF

Love is a flame that burns everything other than itself.
It is the destruction of all that is false
and the fulfillment of all that is true.

In the experience of awakening what's discovered is personal freedom. Personal freedom is freedom from everything that ever happened. It is freedom from identity being confined to the body, mind, memory, and all the ideas that we hold about ourselves. In personal freedom, one has the sense of "I am free." The "I am" has a perfume of the personal. Here, freedom refers to the "I am;" later one will go beyond the "I am."

Once you're finished being enamored with your freedom from all that is personal, there arises a love greater than anything that could be called personal. The dawning of this love within the human heart seeks something far greater than anything previously experienced. It's a love that seeks the liberation of the whole. In that light, personal liberation starts to seem almost petty.

The expansion from personal liberation into a far greater love and concern for that which could never be called personal, is often one of the hardest things for spiritual seekers to come to grips with. This love is so big that often our self-concern and our fascination with our own liberation feel threatened. By "threatened" I mean that it makes such self-concern seem small in the face of something so much bigger.

The Love of which I am speaking, arises directly out of a profound depth of realization. It has nothing to do with doing the right thing or being a good person. Such notions come from an egoic mind masquerading in spiritual clothing. I am speaking about a force of Love that originates from beyond the mind—from consciousness itself.

Q: Is awakening to this greater love the difference between somebody who is fascinated with spirituality and someone who is actually demonstrating spirituality in the way they live?

A: Someone who acts out of fascination is still concerned with some sort of spiritual image or intellectual curiosity. By its very nature a love that is much, much bigger than oneself comes from an entirely different place. It comes from a place of seeing that the Truth seeks to be manifested and expressed through a human personality for the sake of the evolution of the whole. The love I am speaking of comes out of the revelation that you are the whole.

Q: Is this a point at which many people begin to hesitate giving all of themselves?

A: What I'm speaking about is the awakening of a love that makes whatever is happening in oneself unimportant. For such a person self-concern has dropped out of the center of awareness. Enlighten-ment is not only the experience of transcending the me; it's also a condition where the me, as a separate somebody, doesn't hold importance anymore. It doesn't always start out this absolute, but this is the direction non-personal love pushes you toward. Very often at this point, at this juncture, whatever's left of a me who is clinging to itself will start to scream and come up with 101 reasons why it can't yet let go into a love that big.

Q: That's what I'm interested in—that push, that process of unfolding. I would like to hear more about your experience with that process.

A: Ultimately one is either going to say "yes" to that movement of love which is completely non-personal, or to say "no." It may or may not be a long path getting to that point of ultimately saying "yes," but that's exactly what needs to be done. God is only waiting for an unconditional "Yes."

Q: Aren't there starts and stops to that? And a continual choice to say "yes"?

A: The whole idea is to get to the point where it is no longer a minute-to-minute choice. Of course it may be a continual minute-to-minute choice, but the problem is that choosing takes effort. It's always a decision; at each moment you're never sure which way you're going to go. However, there can, and must, come a point when one simply says "yes." Period. You know inside that choice has been made because choice falls away. It ultimately comes down to a black and whiteness that most people have a great amount of difficulty with. Whatever is left of the me always seeks the gray areas. As long as we're seeking gray areas, it means we haven't really come to a reckoning inside with that Love which seeks only itself.

Love is a tremendous caring that arises in the wake of transcending the personal self. In the wake of this transcendence, something amazing arises. A deep love and caring arises from within emptiness, from nowhere. This love and caring seeks only the Truth in every moment and in all circumstances.

True love is something far greater than anything that could be called personal. True love is a non-personal miracle. It is the nature of reality itself. It is the natural and spontaneous expression of the undivided Self.

Q: Some may think you're speaking of a me that learns to be centered on the whole rather than centered on itself. But doesn't the love come from the falling away of the me, the realization that you are not other than the whole?

A: Yes. The love that I'm speaking about is not something that can be created. A love greater than oneself, by its very nature, is something that we can't manufacture. The me cannot manufacture it, even if it wants to. This Love arises from the Self—from realization of the Self.

Q: This love can't even be known when the me is there.

A: Right. At its best it can be intuited. And I think that the intuition of this degree of love magnetically draws the individual toward it and, at the same time, causes fear to arise. This Love is seeking the dissolution of all separateness, all me-ness, all self-concern.

Q: Would developing a more subtle ear for that intuition be helpful?

A: By all means, listen and feel into the intuition of oneness within. The feeling of oneness is love; the experience of oneness is realization of your true nature. Love only seems other than you or bigger than you when you are trapped in the perspective of a personal me. This non-personal love actually *is* you because you, as you truly are, have never been that which is personal. In one sense, it's simply a matter of how deep enlightenment has gone, how thorough it is.

Q: The love, the loving, and the loved, all become one thing.

A: Yes. We can't really love the whole until we have a deep realization that we *are* the whole. Otherwise, the vastness of that love is always going to be experienced as a threat to the me.

Love cares not for the me, it cares only for that which is true, undivided, and whole. When the me dissolves, when it surrenders itself to a unity far greater than anything the mind can comprehend, that is Love.

❀

Q: In this love, is there any validity to the perception that there are blocks in this individual, and measures to take to be more open?

A: The only real block is believing in a me who has blocks. The me is always going to perceive itself as having blocks. The time never comes when the me doesn't perceive itself as having blocks. The biggest block is the mistaken perception that there is a me who has blocks.

❀

Q: Is there any space for emotional feelings in non-personal love?

A: Non-personal love is not a feeling, yet within it there can be, and there is, feeling and emotion. But the feeling and emotion are not derived from a personal me. The feeling and emotion are derived from the absence of a personal me.

Q: Then, would the feelings within non-personal love only be positive feelings?

A: Only a personal me puts feelings into the concept of positive or negative. From the non-personal perspective, feelings are just feelings. Some fall into a category that could be called positive, and others fall into a category that could be called negative. But from the standpoint of the ultimate perspective, those are just arbitrary categories that create division.

Q: Within non-personal love, are feelings experienced but never attached to? It seems that attachment puts me right back into the personal, into separateness.

A: Feelings aren't the point. It's the attachment to the feelings that creates the sense of separation, suffering, and the illusionary me.

In the face of true Love, any holding onto a liberation or freedom that is personal becomes absurd. Love sweeps you up into a mysterious passion and utter commitment to the whole where to live only for oneself is seen as utter madness. The mind does not want to see that this obsession with the personal is madness; it wants to find meaning in it. From the standpoint of Love, all that is false is to be consumed in a passion for the Truth alone.

Q: When I think about the implications of awakening, I think of the Buddhist phrase "saving all beings," but I do not know the exact form that would take in my life.

A: "Saving all beings" is not something that *you* do. Saving all beings is a verb that you become. You become the saving of all beings. That is what you are. In that there is, quite naturally, the very spontaneous and effortless manifestation of love, compassion, wisdom, and a dedication to the Truth above all else. Saving all beings is not what you *do*; it is the definition of what you are.

Q: I've heard you talk about enlightenment as being non-personal, i.e., that the true implications of awakening stretch far beyond the personal. Could you explain what you mean?

A: Personal enlightenment is an exclusive transcendence, in that it excludes the world of space and time. It arrives at eternity by a transcendent exclusion of the relative world of space and time. Non-personal enlightenment is an inclusive transcendence; it sees that the world of space and time *is* the *expression* of eternity. Thus, it is a truly non-dual perspective.

The implications of personal enlightenment are profound, indeed, but the implications of non-personal enlightenment are earth shattering in the most positive sense. Realize that *you are the whole*, and you will see what I mean.

Q: After discovering the vastness of Love, I tried to capture it and understand it. Now I am experiencing an excruciating sense of loss because I am not able to directly experience that all-inclusive Love.

A: So stop looking into it as if it were other than yourself. As long as you look into Love as though it is other than yourself, you will always feel impotent to the task at hand.

Q: Looking into it creates the separation.

A: Yes. Be willing to fathom the possibility that you *are* that love, and simply say "yes" to all that it demands. Don't side with the "no." Don't side with "I can't." See that the love is your Self; then the response to it that says "yes" comes from your deepest nature.

It's a matter of allowing the mind to be humbled, to not know what to do with such a great love. Then, allow yourself to stay that way. That's the key. Don't try to contain it with the mind or even understand it.

Q: That's what I did. I tried to contain it, to understand it.

A: That's not necessary. Just see that you are That, and be it. You don't have to understand it to be it.

Q: I feel so much sadness about Man's cruelty to animals and children. How can I love those who do this?

A: The perspective of Love doesn't leave anybody out. Love even loves those who don't love. The only chance that those who don't love have to change, is to come into contact with that Love.

Q: I used to be angry at God, but now I'm just angry at them.

A: They are God.

Q: It feels as if there is profound responsibility in being Love.

A: Yes, more than the mind could imagine or hold up under. If most human beings truly realized the impact that they have on the whole, they'd be crushed by the realization of it. But what I'm talking about is being thrilled by it. All you have to do is say "yes." Don't make some big project out of it. Don't make some big deal out of it. Just say "yes." You don't even know what it means to say "yes," but you say it anyway. You'll never know what it means to say "yes," but you do it anyway. Freedom and Love arise when you die into the unknown mystery of being.

Nine

WHAT IS LIBERATION?

You are so much less than your experiences,
and therefore so much more.

Liberation is the cessation of the seeker, the seeking, and the sought. It is the end of struggle, separation, and fear. It is beyond all experience and the experiencer thereof. Liberation is what you were born to realize. It is the nature of your own Self.

Q: How is liberation different from realization?

A: Realization is direct experience and insight which can lead to liberation. Realization is that which allows one to truly let go. The result of that letting go is liberation.

We can have many, many spiritual realizations, many spiritual experiences, many deep insights, and still remain very attached to the experience of realization. In this sense, realizations themselves can become forms of addiction. Even deep and profound realizations and spiritual experiences can be co-opted by the mind and become mere objects of fascination.

Liberation is beyond any experience, or any insight. It is the ultimate non-attainment. Realizations are often extraordinary and entertaining. Liberation is ordinary and thorough. As I said, realization can lead to liberation if one completely surrenders into the non-state which deep and profound realization can open you to.

Q: I have heard you say that everything is consciousness. But you also say that liberation is beyond consciousness. Could you explain what you mean?

A: There is only consciousness. There is no individual apart from consciousness who is conscious. The individual is consciousness, and the consciousness that is aware of the individual is consciousness. Whether formless being or in manifest form, all that is, is consciousness.

Before consciousness there is emptiness. Emptiness is neither formless nor has it any form. Emptiness neither exists nor does not exist, for it is beyond all conceptual understanding. Neither the mind, nor the senses, nor consciousness can touch emptiness. Emptiness is the Ultimate Principle, the Self, the Source of all. That awareness of consciousness is emptiness.

When you go to sleep at night you are no longer conscious, but there is awareness. When you sleep, consciousness is no more; being-ness is no more; oneness is no more. And yet, *you* still are. What is that?

Q: When I am asleep I am not aware of anything.

A: Who says this? How do you know that you are not aware? You must be aware that you are not aware. Who is that awareness who says that I am not aware?

Q: When I wake up, I have no memory of being aware during sleep.

A: Yet when you wake up, you are the same person who went to sleep. Something continued through the night, something more than the body, mind, or memory. If there was no continual awareness, the body would wake up and you would not know who you are. Memory is nothing without awareness. Awareness is the first principle. Pay attention to it, and it will grow in intensity throughout all states. Do not tie your freedom to what comes and goes. Liberation is the discovery that you are That which always is. But to understand what I say is not enough, you must *be* it—knowingly.

Q: What motivates a liberated person to act in the world? It seems that without the motivation of desire, even the desire to help others, there would be no motivation to act at all.

A: In Liberation you are in that state which is prior to any causation. Therefore, actions happen without any motivation for doing them. You are not doing for yourself or for the love of others. You are prior to any motivation. Actions simply happen. From the outside, such actions may be viewed as loving, kind, and wise, but to the liberated one, all happens spontaneously and free of any motive. Actions arise out of the most natural, primordial state.

Q: So why do you come and give satsang?

A: I have no idea. In the morning the sun rises, in the evening it sets again. Seekers have questions, which give rise to the teacher and the teaching.

Q: I have heard you talk about non-personal enlightenment and a deep love for the whole. How does that fit in with having no motivation?

A: First, one awakens to personal freedom: the realization that you are formless consciousness itself. As consciousness, you are free of body-mind identity. Then, there is the awakening to non-personal freedom. This is the birth of a vast non-personal Love for the whole, for all beings and all things. It is the realization that *you are the whole.* Therefore, a freedom that is in any sense personal seems pale in comparison to a love, which is so much greater. This is a phase of surrendering any and all personal attachments to the greatest good, the Self. As self-centered concerns dissolve, a love that is all-inclusive sweeps you up into its arms and into a new life of service, celebration, and love.

With the dawning of Liberation, all motivations drop away. One does not act out of any reason or motivation, action simply occurs. Many mistake personal freedom for liberation because in personal freedom it is common to lose self-centered motivations to act. Many get stuck there thinking that they are in the highest state, but they are actually stuck in the emptiness, or absence, of self-centered motivations. They have not yet awakened to a truly selfless, non-personal love and life of service.

Beyond non-personal freedom lies Liberation. A liberated person has transcended any motivations, personal or non-personal. Everything happens spontaneously, free of any sense of being the doer of deeds. The liberated one has association with consciousness but does not dwell there. The liberated one has returned consciously to the ultimate principle, which resides before the consciousness. He is the awareness of consciousness. Evolution has taken place in him.

⚛

Q: Is there a time when vigilance can finally be put down?

A: Both vigilance and no vigilance refer to a "me." One refers to "*I* must be vigilant," and the other refers to "now *I* don't have to be vigilant." Liberation is freedom from both extremes. The concepts of vigilance and non-vigilance don't apply.

Q: Does this mean that landing is not possible from this place?

A: By landing I assume you mean fixating or holding on to some experience, insight, or state.

As soon as you say something is not possible, you have opened a gate for it to not only become possible, but highly probable.

⚛

Q: What is liberated from what?

A: That sort of question is what you're liberated from. Be sincere; don't ask questions out of mere interest. Ask dangerous questions—the ones whose answers could change your life.

Q: It seems that suffering is the source of the desire for liberation. Is it the embracing of suffering, then, that is the key to liberation?

A: If by embracing suffering you mean to not avoid it, then yes, embrace it, but do not indulge in it. Embrace the suffering so that you can go beyond it. Ask yourself: Who suffers? Who embraces?

There are lots of people who suffer and don't desire liberation. The desire for liberation comes into the sense of a separate me from outside of that me. It's an evolutionary impulse that either is or isn't awakened. The impulse to be free may use suffering in order to accomplish its task, but it does not need suffering to do so. There is no great significance or purpose to suffering. Suffering is a waste of your time. If you are suffering, you are not perceiving the Truth. Seek the true and right perspective on things, starting with yourself.

Those who are free don't want anything. They don't want anything from their mind, they don't want anything from their emotions, they don't want anything from anyone, and they don't want anything from life. They don't want anything. If you don't want, all that's left is an incredible sense of being free.

Q: Isn't liberation ultimate stopping or resting? If one never lands, what does that life look like?

A: Liberation is not *stopping*; it's *cessation*. The two are very different. Cessation means extinction. It means the death of identification. Stopping implies no motion, while cessation is the end of struggle. Stopping is what you do when the traffic light turns red. Cessation of struggle is like free-falling through space without a care in the world.

When realization matures, you have realization but there's nothing there to reflect on it. So, quite naturally, there's a sobriety to realization. That's why sages throughout time have said that the deepest realization is beyond experience—because there is no one left to be whooping and hollering about it. This is the attainment of non-attainment.

Q: I'm curious, is there any perception of difficulty for you?

A: There is neither difficulty nor not difficulty. Things are simply the way they are. Liberation is a complete acceptance of what is. Accept everything, and you will no longer be tied to anything. Whatever you accept, you go beyond. Liberation is complete acceptance and, therefore, complete transcendence.

Whatever you accept, you go beyond. If you accept everything, you go beyond everything. Going beyond the world, you are free to be *in* it because you are the world. The knowingness that you are all-that-is, that knowingness itself, is beyond the world, beyond consciousness, beyond all. The truly liberated one has transcended even the oneness of consciousness, as if being in deep sleep but fully awake.

Q: If there is no goal, nothing to change, and no answer to attain, what is the appropriate attitude to bring to the inquiry?

A: All inquiry is meant for one purpose: to take you experientially into the Unknown as efficiently as possible. Once you get there, simply be still because the inquiry has delivered you to its destination. The rest is up to Grace.

Do not hold onto any knowledge that comes your way. Even the greatest revelations must not be clung to, or you will end up with a head full of memories and a heart empty of substance. The truth is ever new, existing only in the now. The highest truth is beyond knowledge and experience. It is beyond time and space, and beyond being-ness, consciousness, and oneness.

Q: Is your awareness as final and complete as it ever will or possibly can be?

A: There is no final, and no other than final.

Q: It transcends all that because those are concepts?

A: When you realize what and who you are, completely, absolutely, and thoroughly, there's no doubt at all, and therefore, no suffering. Suffering no longer exists for that person because they are no longer struggling with a conceptual me who is in opposition to what is. The separate me is transcended. Even consciousness is transcended. That is a liberated person. Liberated from the igno-rance of misunderstanding. This is enormous in its implications for consciousness as a whole because every time one person realizes the Self, consciousness as a whole has evolved.

Q: So different realms open up?

A: All realms are on the surface. No matter how subtle the psychic realm or the spiritual realm—it's all manifestation. When you wake up to who you are, all manifestation is transcended. No realms are any better than any other realms, ultimately. All realms are manifestation and therefore illusion. The deepening is something that can't be talked about. First find out who you are, then you'll find yourself sinking into an infinite ocean. You will be as if in deep sleep, yet fully aware and functional.

Q: What we term "the direct path" seems to utilize techniques—not to purify an individual self, but rather, to make it apparent that that self simply does not exist. How can one not lose sight of the purpose of these techniques?

A: Just remember that all direct path techniques are meant simply to undermine, to cut away, the one who is performing them.

No matter what spiritual path you've walked or what teachings you've followed, they must lead you back to no path and no teaching. A true teaching is like a blazing fire that consumes itself. The teaching must not only consume you, but consume itself as well. All must be burned to ash, and then the ash must be burned. Then, and only then, is the Ultimate realized.

Q: Is there any point at which the question "What is liberation?" burns itself out?

A: When liberation is achieved, there is no longer the question "What is liberation?" There is only primordial openness.

Q: Is that what elicits the wonder?

A: Openness *is* wonder.

True Enlightenment destroys enlightenment. As long as you can refer back to yourself and say, "I'm enlightened," you're not. Enlightenment is authentic only when there is no one left to be enlightened. Even to say, "I am nobody," is one too many.

There's a point when you intuitively realize that to be Free you have to give up your attachment to Freedom. You have to quit asking yourself: Is it still there? Am I okay? You have to decide to never look over your shoulder again to see if you're Free or if others know you're Free. You just have to let yourself burn there—no matter what.

This isn't something I can help you with. I can tell you what you need to do, but you have to do it. In the beginning, teachers can help a lot. But the deeper you go, all they can do is point, and clarify, and tell you what you need to do. Only you can take this step. Nobody can push you into this place.

It's like Buddha's final night under the Bodhi tree. What did he do when confronted with this? He reached down and touched the ground and said, "I will not be moved." Finally—when everything that could be thrown at him was thrown, and he was still unmoved—it was done. He never looked back.

≈

Before you awaken to what you are,
ten thousand words
and a myriad of spiritual experiences
will not be enough.

After you awaken,
just one is too much.

≈

Ten

THE STUDENT-TEACHER RELATIONSHIP

Yearning is the seed of Freedom.
The student is the soil, and the teacher is the rain.
Liberation is the harvest.

Q: What is the spiritual teacher's role in life?

A: To be themselves. That *is* the teacher's teaching. The true spiritual teacher is that rare being who does not play roles.

Q: And what is the role of the spiritual student?

A: The role of the spiritual student is to seek the demise of the role of spiritual student—as quickly as possible.

～

Do not just listen to what I say, feel what I say within yourself.
To feel what I say is most important.
Through the feeling of it you will be taken beyond.

～

Q: Where is the line between respect and trust for the teacher vs. pretending that the teacher can do no wrong?

A: Forget pretending that the teacher can do no wrong. This sort of immature projection is what seekers do as a way of avoiding responsibility for themselves. One should never give their good sense away, and if they do, it's their own fault. Mature respect and trust are always earned. If a student gives them immediately, this is not only immature, but also dangerous. It's a sign that the student is not seeking the Truth, but is actually seeking a mother or father figure—someone to tell them what to do and to relieve them of the insecurity of not knowing what the Truth actually is.

Q: It seems that some projection is inevitable, even on the part of the responsible student. Other than just being aware of this, how can the student deal with that issue?

A: The student, with the help of the teacher, first needs to be aware of, or made aware of, the projection. Many students don't want the teacher to point this out because it robs them of their most cherished illusions that they use to protect themselves from their own insecurities. So first, you have to be open to seeing a projection as a projection. A true teacher will not intentionally use any projection for any reason. If the student holds onto it and finds some temporary usefulness in it, that's his own doing. The true teacher simply is who he or she is, and does not get involved in the game of projections. You'll find that the true teacher, whether you have projections or not, does not alter the way they behave toward you at all. If they do, run the other way as fast as you can.

Do not seek comfort from the spiritual teacher;
seek only the Truth itself.

A: Most people come to satsang to hear what I have to say. I ought to give them popcorn and coke and send them off to the movies. It would be cheaper, and the seats are more comfortable.

Q: So why should we come here to satsang?

A: Because your heart wants to burst open, your mind wants to crack, and you are ready to die for freedom.

❀

Q: How can a student most effectively utilize a spiritual teacher for the speediest and most complete demise of the ego?

A: The teacher is not merely the one who stands before you. That is only the teacher's form. That which is *animating* the form called "teacher" is the true Self of the teacher. See that your teacher is that which is animating the form called "teacher." What is that which animates form?

Utilize the form called teacher to find the ultimate principle that is animating all forms, including yourself. Then see that ultimate principle as your own Self, as everything that is.

❀

Q: How does one purely express devotion that is devoid of projection?

A: True devotion has no projection. Otherwise it's being devoted to a fantasy, to an image. This is better known as worship. Worshipping is when you put any head above your own. This is simply ignorance and causes further and further separation. Devotion comes out of an intuitive sense of unity or oneness. This oneness can be the source of great devotion and great love. But if your devotion makes you feel separate from the object of your devotion, you have fallen into the ignorance of worship.

When you truly allow the teacher's presence into yourself, that presence will stay with you even when you are not with the teacher in form. The teacher's presence will be with you always, and the teaching will continue to come from that presence. This is called the transmission of the teaching. Once you let the transmission in, everything happens spontaneously, but you must trust it more than you trust your mind and your fears.

Q: Ramana did much of his teaching in silence, and I am aware that you are teaching me this way; somehow it's transmitting to me without words. Yet, often the words are important in helping my mind understand. Will you comment on silent teachings vs. spoken teachings?

A: Spoken teachings are meant to orient you to deeper truths about yourself and to provide an intellectual context into which the mind can relax. This relaxation of the mind is ultimately the aim of any spoken teaching. Unspoken teachings arise out of Presence, out of Silence, and may or may not contain words. These teachings are the most powerful and profound and also lead to deeper and deeper silence. In working with a teacher, the aim is to first internalize the teacher's Presence and teaching inside yourself. Eventually, you and the internal Presence of the teacher begin to merge and become one and the same. Only then is it truly perceived that the teacher's Presence was your own Self all along. It is not necessary, and is even unwise, to hold onto the form of the teacher or to internalize the image you have of the teacher. What I am speaking about is the Presence of the teacher. That Presence takes you beyond to the Self.

~

Before I took this birth I decided to give up all powers
so that I could show beings how to live by love alone.

~

Q: I've heard a lot about transmission from teacher to student. It's in almost every tradition. What does transmission mean? What gets transmitted?

A: A true teacher is one who opens space within your mind. If you turn your attention away from everything else and merge with that space, you awaken as that consciousness. This space is the true teacher's gift. It is an open door, but you must walk through it. Surrender to the space within yourself that the teacher awakens. Emptiness is the true teacher's transmission. Surrender to that alone, and you will discover limitless fullness of being.

Q: How big a part does the teacher's transmission play in the realization of who one is?

A: All words spoken by the teacher are simply meant to get the mind to relax enough so that the transmission can get in. The transmission is the teaching. It is the passing of the flame. When the flame of transmission ignites fully within your heart, that is Self realization.

Q: What is the transmission?

A: Transmission is a mystery. It is not something that the teacher controls, manipulates, or even intends. It is spontaneous. It has a wisdom all its own that is unfathomable.

Q: Is it the same as shakti?

A: No. Shakti is spiritual candy. Many spiritual seekers become attached to a teacher's shakti, to their energy. But true transmission is not an experience, emotion, or state.

Sincere students find sincere teachers, and sincere teachers find sincere students. The two go together like a box and its lid.

Q: I am interested in addressing the issue of the negotiating that some students do with their teachers, when they want the teacher to act, or react, or be a certain way.

A: A true teacher does not negotiate. A true teacher manifests the highest Truth. That is his only concern. Through the teacher's reflection of Truth, students have the opportunity to see where they are negotiating with the Truth within themselves. In order to be free, all negotiation must come to an end.

Q: What attitude toward a true teacher is the most effective for the non-personal process termed "awakening"?

A: The correct attitude is one where you have no more time to waste. This means that everything is oriented toward the now. The correct attitude is that there is no such thing as an awakening that happens tomorrow. Tomorrows never come. The time is now. You must be sincere. Sincerity and earnestness are the most beneficial attitudes to have.

Q: How does one know if they've met their teacher and if that is their teacher for life?

A: There's nothing of the mind that will tell you that you have met your teacher. It's a matter of intuition. It's a knowingness, beyond any emotion or any feeling. It's simply a knowing, "Yes, this is the one." Once you have found your true teacher, that finding is outside of time. It has nothing to do with lasting one's entire life. The true teacher puts an end to your illusion of time, so that tomorrow is no longer a consideration. The true student is not bound to their teacher by loyalty or obligation, but by love and respect.

Q: Does loyalty to a teacher ever get in the way?

A: The true teacher does not need the student's loyalty. Loyalty is a substitute for love, trust, and respect. Without these, there is simply no reason to be with any teacher. Loyalty plays no part.

Q: Even to the student?

A: Students do not need loyalty; they need earnestness, sincerity, and courage. The true teacher only wants what's best for you.

Q: Most students believe that the teacher is more awake or more aware than the students are. Given this belief, how can any student ever have a teacher who he doesn't become attached to or dependent upon?

A: The relationship between teacher and student is precisely for the purpose of removing this very illusion. Most students come to a spiritual teacher with certain dependencies. This is to be expected. However, if the relationship with the teacher is based upon these dependencies, then it is doomed to failure. Like a child who is dependent upon its mother but later grows beyond that dependency, the student should, from the very start, be endeavoring to grow beyond their dependency on the spiritual teacher. This is a very delicate and subtle process that requires a very sincere student and a very clear teacher.

∼

I am the unknowingness
of an unknown mystery.
If you want to know something,
go elsewhere.
If you want to un-know everything,
then sit and listen.

The silence inside of you
is the sound of your knowledge collapsing.
Remember, it is you who said,
"I want to be free."

∼

Eleven

RELATIONSHIP

True relationship is not what happens between two or more entities.
True relationship is the Oneness dancing with Itself.

It is important when we consider the subject of relationship, that we not limit our consideration only to relationship between human beings, but broaden it to include our relationship to the whole of life. From the ego's limited point of view, relationship is always between objects—between a personal "me" and something other than me. It is from this limited point of view that most human beings begin their consideration of what enlightened relationship is. However, in order to find out what enlightened relationship is, it is imperative that the ego's reality as a separate entity be questioned. Because as long as we perceive our self to be a separate ego, enlightened relationship to others and to life as a whole will remain impossibilities.

Q: When I think of what my relationship is with life, I find I want to avoid daily challenges. My hope is that, when I become enlightened, life will be easier for me.

A: If you want to be free, you cannot hide from anything. Many spiritual seekers are using spiritual practices as a means to avoid many aspects of themselves. The problem with this is that as long as you are avoiding anything, you are not living in truth. You are avoiding truth. No one ever became enlightened by avoiding truth.

If you want to be free, then you must face yourself and face your life as it is. Do not use spirituality or spiritual experience as something to hide behind. As long as you are avoiding parts of yourself, or life in general, then even very profound spiritual experiences and revelations will have very little permanent effect on you. Do not simply seek to transcend life, but realize that you are all of Life. You are Life itself.

Q: What is the right relationship to have with spiritual experiences?

A: What's important about spiritual experiences is how you relate to them. Two people can relate very differently to the same experience. One can be set free as a result of profound spiritual experience, while another will cling to old habits of conditioning, attachment, and ego. Everything depends upon your readiness and willingness to let go into the Unknown, and live from that mysterious and precious condition. The question is: Are you ready to give up everything when God comes knocking at your door? This willingness to completely let go and surrender to the divine determines how free you will ultimately become. Whatever you hold back for yourself will become your prison. My advice is to give your whole heart, mind, body, and soul to Grace when it comes. Ask yourself *now*: Am I ready?

If one is to be truly free, then one must truly want to be free of all attachments, aversions and dependencies upon others to meet their emotional and psychological needs. This is challenging indeed to many seekers.

Q: Is there such a thing as being in an intimate relationship that consciously supports the other towards freedom?

A: If by "support" you mean "encourages the freedom of another," then this is the very essence of a relationship founded in Truth. However, many seek support in relationships as compensation for their own lack of earnestness and dedication to the Truth. This dependency, which masquerades as support, is something that many spiritual seekers ask of their partners because they have not yet found it within themselves. Support, as it relates to Truth, is more like a hand held open in which someone can unfold if they desire. It is not compensation.

Relationship based on Truth, which means a relationship that is free of dependency and demands, is a relationship centered upon celebration. It's a mutual coming together for no other reason than being together.

Deeply inquiring into the question "Who is another?" can lead to the direct experience that the other is one's own Self—that in fact, there is no other. However, I have seen that for most seekers, even this experiential revelation is not enough to transform the painfully personal ways that they relate.

To come to this profound transformation requires a very deep investigation of the implications inherent in the experiential revelation that there is no other. It is in the daily living of these implications that most seekers fail. Why? Because, fundamentally, most people want to remain separate and in control. Simply put, most people want to keep dreaming that they are special, unique, and separate. They want to remain separate more than they want to wake up to the perfect unity of an Unknown which leaves no room for any separation from the whole.

As long as you perceive that anyone is holding you back, you have not taken full responsibility for your own liberation. Liberation means that you stand free of making demands on others and on life to make you happy. When you discover yourself to be nothing but Freedom, you stop setting up conditions and requirements that need to be satisfied in order for you to be happy. It is in the absolute surrender of all conditions and requirements that Liberation is discovered to be who and what you Are. Then the love and wisdom that flow out of you have a liberating effect on others.

Q: Don't we have a responsibility to expose each other's faults, to assist in growth and overcoming blind spots?

A: Many people think the purpose of relationship is to work out their stuff, but I don't think that's what relationships are for. I think working out your stuff is your own job, not the relationship's. You work yourself out. You're alone in finding Freedom, in finding the Beloved. That's up to you. When you're clear on this, relationship can flower. If you aren't, then you're always using each other to work stuff out, and you become two tools: I point out your junk, you point out mine, and we pretend like that's a good thing.

Awakening to the truth of Unity means to awaken from the dream of a personal self and personal others, to the realization that there is no other. Many spiritual seekers have had glimpses of the absolute Unity of all existence, but few are capable of or willing to live up to the many challenging implications inherent in that revelation. The revelation of Unity, that there is no other, is a realization of the ultimate non-personal nature of all that seems so very personal. Applying this realization to the arena of personal relationships is something that most seekers find extremely challenging. This is the number one reason why so many seekers never come completely to rest in the freedom of the Self Absolute.

Q: I just finished talking with a friend of mine who was very depressed, and I felt good about how I handled it. But now, I notice that I feel depleted.

A: Did you see the depression as a problem?

Q: Yes. I saw it as a problem to her.

A: Truth has a very objective way of perceiving just these kinds of personal situations, because it always seeks the Truth and nothing else. It doesn't seek feeling good; it seeks the Truth.

Q: It seems like I handled it like you would have, but it didn't go right past me as it would have for you, or else I wouldn't feel drained.

A: The reason that it would have gone right past me is that I know that it's not a problem, and I have no investment in helping that person.

Q: But you would help.

A: My response wouldn't come out of a motivation to help; it would come out of the Self. The Self seeks the Truth. The Self is the Truth, and the Truth seeks itself.

When you're dealing with someone else, motivation is what counts. If the motivation is for Truth, then it's clean and you don't feel drained. However, if the motivation, either consciously or unconsciously, isn't for Truth but is to help, then there's a stickiness which is draining. Looking back on it, was your motivation clean and unattached?

Q: Because it was depleting, it must not have been. There must have been some attachment there.

A: The attachment was your investment in the result. If you're not personally invested in the result, you won't get tired.

Q: What is the role and value of Sangha (spiritual community)?

A: I don't think of the Sangha as having a role. I think that that would be making a demand upon the Sangha that doesn't belong to it.

Q: What is the relationship of the spiritual seeker to the Sangha?

A: There is a freedom that can be discovered in relationship, whether it be with spiritual community or with another individual, where something much bigger than any individual is born. What I am speaking about is an intimacy that flowers in the presence of

Truth. The depth of this intimacy can be a vehicle through which oneness is experienced. For some, this degree of intimacy is positive beyond belief; for others, it is the cause of mistrust and fear. True intimacy always threatens the sense of separateness.

Q: How can I save my children from identification with the personal self and the suffering that it entails?

A: It's not a problem, just like being a child isn't a problem. When we become adults, we don't look back and say, "Well, being a child was a complete waste of time!" We leave being a child behind, but we don't assume it was a mistake. The personal self is not our adversary but simply something we leave behind and go beyond. Unfortunately, few people go beyond the separate sense of I. When the time is right, your child will start to question the sense of I. Keep this inquiry open for your child by keeping it open and alive within yourself.

Q: You have spoken of a third entity called "relationship." Can you speak about what this is?

A: The third entity is the oneness that shines through when two are in selfless relationship. No longer is the relationship the primary focus; instead, it is the oneness that perfumes each moment of it. True relationship not only elicits this oneness, but it is dedicated to it above all else. So when you're truly meeting, it is the one essence that shines through.

Q: Is this the same experience that I've noticed in large groups where I recognize a flavor of oneness that varies from group to group?

A: When I say "oneness," I am not speaking so much about a flavor of oneness, which a group of people may share. I'm speaking about the perception that the other is myself, and about the joy and love that arises from this perception.

Q: How might sex in romantic relationship and sexuality within oneself be affected by enlightenment?

A: With the dawning of enlightenment, sex either happens or it doesn't, but it is no longer the central focus of relationship. The oneness is the focus, and sex can either continue or not continue depending upon the destiny of the individuals involved. One stops defining the relationship by the content of its sexuality.

Q: Is there someone each of us is destined to be with?

A: If you are destined to be with somebody, you will be. Why bother with the question?

Q: I think I bother with the question to gain a sense of hope.

A: Do not tie your happiness to others. You yourself contain abundant happiness. Look under your hopelessness and find the source of yourself. Seek your Self and all else will be taken care of.

Q: I was deeply in tune with a teacher and contented within myself. Then, without planning it or thinking about it, celibacy happened of its own accord. Was this an escape from relationship and human sexuality? Later, when I suddenly had physical and sensual urges again, did I suddenly leave love and its fulfilling contentment?

A: Everything has its time and place. At one time you can be naturally called to celibacy, and at another called to non-celibacy. Each can have its purpose and need not be judged. Whether or not one is celibate means absolutely nothing. Do not deny or indulge; simply follow your nature. This is the best course of action.

Q: I'm curious what you have to say about the relationship of humanity with the environment of the planet.

A: The hope for the environment does not lie in the hands of the environmentalists. They simply sit on the opposite side of the duality from those who destroy the environment. They are culprits in continuing a type of violence that is the very root of what causes us to destroy the environment. The hope for the environment lies in the realization that all beings and all things are yourself, including those who oppose you. Until your vision and compassion is big enough to include those who oppose you, you are simply contributing to the continuation of destructiveness. The end of separation is the salvation for all.

Twelve

THE COURAGE TO QUESTION

Keep questioning right down to the marrow,
until the questioner dissolves—
leaving only a passing draft
where there was once a solid illusion called me.

Most people come to spiritual teachers and teachings with a host of hidden beliefs, ideas, and assumptions that they unconsciously seek to be confirmed. Even if they are willing to question these beliefs they almost always replace the old concepts with new, more spiritual ones—thinking that these new concepts are far more real than the old ones.

Even those who have had deep spiritual experiences and awakenings beyond the mind will, in most cases, continue to cling to superstitious ideas and beliefs. This is an unconscious effort to grasp for the security of the known, the accepted, or the expected. It is this grasping for security, in all its inner and outer forms, that limits the perspective of enlightenment and maintains an inwardly divided condition which is the cause of all suffering and confusion. In order to fully awaken to the fact that you are nothing but Awakeness itself, you must want to know the truth more than you want to feel secure.

Shortly after I began teaching, I noticed that almost everyone coming to see me held a tremendous number of superstitious ideas and beliefs that were distorting their perceptions and limiting their scope of spiritual inquiry. What was most surprising was that even those who had had deep and profound experiences of spiritual awakening continued to hold onto superstitious ideas and beliefs which severely limited their depth of experience and expression of true awakening. Over time, I began to see how delicate and challenging it was for most seekers to find the courage to question any and all ideas and beliefs about the true nature of themselves, the world, others, and even enlightenment itself.

In almost every person, every religion, every group, every teaching, and every teacher, there are ideas, beliefs, and assumptions, which are overtly or covertly not open to question. Often these unquestioned beliefs hide superstitions, which are protecting something that is untrue, contradictory, or being used as justification for teachings and behaviors that are less than enlightened.

The challenge of enlightenment is not simply to glimpse the awakened conditioned, nor even to continually experience it. It is to be and express it as your self in the way you move in the world. In order to do this, you must come out of hiding behind any superstitious beliefs and find the courage to question everything. Otherwise, you will continue to hold onto superstitions that distort your perception and expression of that which is only ever AWAKE.

ABOUT THE AUTHOR

Inspired by a powerful spiritual awakening, and in response to the request of his teacher, Adyashanti passionately shares his unique teaching with all who desire the freedom of Liberation. Adyashanti's teaching embodies the non-dual realization of both Zen and Advaita Vedanta. It is a clear, original, and comprehensive expression of the enlightened condition. Adyashanti dares all seekers of peace and freedom to take the possibility of Liberation in this life seriously.

For more information about satsangs, intensives, and retreats with Adyashanti, please visit our web site, www.zen-satsang.org, or write to:

Open Gate Sangha, Inc.
P.O. Box 782
Los Gatos, California 95031 USA